Jofrid Gunn

BY THE SAME AUTHOR

Josephine Tey: A Life
Daughters of the North: Jean Gordon and Mary, Queen of Scots

Jofrid Gunn

Jennifer Morag Henderson

Shearsman Books

First published in the United Kingdom in 2025 by
Shearsman Books Ltd
PO Box 4239
Swindon
SN3 9FN

Shearsman Books Ltd Registered Office
30–31 St. James Place, Mangotsfield, Bristol BS16 9JB
(this address not for correspondence)

EU AUTHORISED REPRESENTATIVE:
Lightning Source France
1 Av. Johannes Gutenberg, 78310 Maurepas, France
Email: compliance@lightningsource.fr

www.shearsman.com

ISBN 978-1-84861-995-1

Copyright © Jennifer Morag Henderson, 2025

The right of Jennifer Morag Henderson to be identified as the author of this work has been asserted by her in accordance with the Copyrights, Designs and Patents Act of 1988.
All rights reserved.

ACKNOWLEDGEMENTS

Some of these poems have previously been published in *Northwords Now, Causeway / Cabhsair* (Aberdeen University Press), *Poetry Scotland*, and in *The SpecBook 2024* (Speculative Books).

CONTENTS

Memory and Thought	9
Kennings for the sea	10
The Princess of Suðuroy	12
The Skjaldur of the Violin of Jofrid's Wedding	17
An echo is the language of the mountains	18
The Dancing in the Hall	19
Outside	21
Angles	22
Silvertongue	23
Wedding ring shawl	24
I dream about your death	26
Uncontainable	27
The Song	28
[It happened so long ago it's not true anymore]	29
Sodden light	30
Sea Stacks	31
This is a Feigdarferð, doomed sea journey	32
[A silent sunset]	33
Out of Place	34
A lullaby for his daughter	35
Sólja	36
Juniper	37
The Hammerbeam Roof at Darnaway Castle, Moray	39
The Parting Hymn	40
A Riotous Serious Garden	41
Moss	42
[a poem like the curves of the stone]	43
The Mother Troll	44
Other Mothers	46
[the wood is pathless]	47
The Geese flew in a V-shape overhead	48
an impossible island	49
Breathing	50
[the memorial stone stands]	51

Stops	52
Up and down	54
The Clan Gunn's stories	55
The Burial Party	58
Unmoored	60
shore-dweller	61
Creagh-Drumi-Doun	62
Ancestors	65
Intent, discourage, follow, falter	66
Froth	67
The Votive Ship	68
The Original Jofrid	69
Robert Gordon and the burning of the papers of the Earl of Caithness	71
Pulse	73
He wrote asking for a suit of scarlet and grey	74
Bride	75
A plea for understanding and remembrance: wishing to have disputes settled	76
Boat Burning	77
[the travelling never stops]	78
The Violin	79
The Salt and the Coal	82
The Battle of Kringen / Sinklar's Visa	83
children of ash and elm	86
Horizon Calendar in the Astronomical Twilight	88
Scattered Words	89
Time Ocean Water Deep	91
Open light	92
Broken Chronicle	93
Notes	94

Jofrid Gunn

Memory and Thought

Towards the evening, Thought on one shoulder
And Memory weighing on the other
The fire flickers, faces half-shadowed
As the old stories begin to unfold.

Outside the circle, I sit to listen
Hear the wheels of others' lives set spinning
Roses on the hill, rare, pale pink, thorned stems
And Burnt Njal's ghost in the dying embers.

Swords and poets' songs, sad men and women
Others who, like me, are far from their dwelling
Long, complicated, looping histories
The endless nodding genealogies.

I stand, walk shorewards to tell, say in a whisper
To the birds, I am my own chronicler.

Kennings for the sea

I came in on the sea-road
the sail road, the ships' path

The oarstroke-lands
the ring of islands taking me to
a wedding ring
the island ring

from the necklace of the Faroe Islands
away from the plain of puffins
along the water way, the ship's way

sailing through a land of wonders
the broad gunwale road
the gull's land
the whale's land,
the bed of fish
along the roads of the redfish
to the land of the salmon

through the known fishing stations,
the fish-field to the cool plot,
the wave world to a sea of nightmares
the melted ice world
the land of the surge
and trembling ground
the high wave enclosure
of the earth-belt

to the roaring field of the whale
the water-monster's stronghold
truly in the outlying land of the ship
where it earns its name the blood of land

the storm-twisted enclosure
the roaring-beach of the trolling-line.

Then slipped, calmer now
to the enclosure of seaweed
the kelp's land
the ground of Scotland
a new homestead of the prow

follow the birds' track
the marshland of seagulls
the bed of coal-fish

the chain of lands keeps me here
the hollows of the herring
the swollen hall of sands
the boat-land
the deceit-ring

the island fetter

The Princess of Suðuroy

This is the story of the Princess of Suðuroy. Now, the Princess of Suðuroy is a name that is known in the Faroe Islands, where she came to live, but not so well known in Scotland, where she was from. This is the story of how the Princess came to leave Scotland for the Faroes, and what happened when her father, the King of Scots, came to call her home.

The King of Scots was called James. James' own father had been killed in battle, and James had become king when he was very young, only one year old. He was brought up by his mother, and by the important noblemen of the kingdom, but all of them had their own ideas on how to run the country, and they all tried to control King James.

King James grew up to be handsome and clever, as all good kings should be, and he tried hard to escape from the influence of the court around him and to understand his country and the people who lived there. Often, he would cast aside the beautiful red and gold clothes that a king normally wore, and instead put on the clothes of an ordinary Scotsman: dressed like this, he travelled in secret around the country, calling himself the Gudeman (or Good-man) of Ballengeich. As the Gudeman of Ballengeich, he would join ordinary farmers and townspeople at their meals, and learn from their conversation.

One time, when King James was travelling in the far north of Scotland dressed as the Gudeman of Ballengeich, he met a beautiful young lady, and, since all kings and all men have their weaknesses, soon the beautiful young lady was pregnant. She gave birth to a daughter, and it was this daughter who grew up to be the Princess of Suðuroy.

When she was little, the Princess lived with her mother in the far north of Scotland, under the protection of the Clan Gunn. Although she did not live at the court, she knew her father the king, for every year King James toured his kingdom, and every year he would dress as the Gudeman of Ballengeich and come to visit the Princess and the Princess' mother. King James told the Princess that one day she would come and live with him at the court in Edinburgh, and that she would marry a fine nobleman and be rich and make him proud.

But the Princess did not want to live at the court in Edinburgh, or marry a fine nobleman. She wanted to live where she felt free and happy, roaming the hills and coastline of her home in the north, with her best friend, the young boy John Sinclair. Although John was a son of the Sinclair family, he had been sent to be fostered with the Clan Gunn when he was a baby, as the custom was in those days. The idea was that if the Clan Gunn brought up a Sinclair child, then the Sinclairs and the Clan Gunn would become more friendly, and the ancient rivalry that existed between the two families would lessen. But these ideas do not always work, and John Sinclair was not always happy in the Clan Gunn. And because the Princess also was not always very happy – because people would always ask her about her father – soon the Princess and John Sinclair became the best of friends.

And soon enough, the Princess and John Sinclair grew up, and realised that they were in love, and that they wanted to get married. And it happened to be one of the times that King James was visiting, and, as usual, he came to see the Princess and her mother, dressed in his disguise of the Gudeman of Ballengeich. The Princess told her father how she felt about John Sinclair, and asked for his blessing for her marriage.

But King James was very angry. He did not want his daughter the Princess to marry John Sinclair. He wanted his daughter to marry a rich nobleman, and live at court. King James told the Princess that she would not marry John Sinclair, and that she should pack her bags and be ready to leave with him the next morning, when they would travel together to Edinburgh, where she would start a new life at the court.

The Princess packed her bags, but she did not wait til morning. While King James was with her mother, she took her bags and crept out of the house, and went straight to the house of John Sinclair. She woke him up, and she explained to him what her father King James had said, and how he did not want them to marry. John Sinclair said that they must, in that case, get married straight away, so the two young people went straight away to the minister, and since the minister had known them both since they were children and knew that they were in love, he was happy to marry them that very night.

The next morning, when King James found out what had happened, he was furious. The minister came quickly to John Sinclair's house and told him that he and the Princess must leave immediately, because otherwise the King might kill him. So the Princess and John Sinclair ran down to the shore, where John kept his boat, and together they pushed it off the grey stones and into the sea, and they raised the sail and sailed away as fast as the wind would take them.

John was a good sailor, and they sailed for a long time, searching for somewhere that they would be safe, and eventually they came to the Faroe Islands. Now, at that time the Plague had visited the Faroe Islands, and had killed many, many people, and there were a good number of houses standing empty. The Princess and John Sinclair were not afraid of the Plague – or, at least, they were less afraid of the Plague than they were of King James – so they settled in one of the abandoned houses on the island of Suðuroy, the southernmost of the Faroe Islands. Here, the Princess and John Sinclair repaired a small croft building, rebuilding the stone walls and fashioning the roof from turf in the Faroese way, and bringing the land round about it back into cultivation. They knew that the place was blessed when they found a small spring of fresh water just by the door of their new home. But they did not forget Scotland, and when the Princess and John Sinclair sowed the ground round about their house the Princess found a certain type of grass that she had seen growing in the Clan Gunn's lands, and she coaxed it to grow all along a southern-facing slope near Hov, to remind them of their home before they had come north.

The Princess and John Sinclair and their story soon became known in the Faroes, and that is how the Princess became known as 'The Princess of Suðuroy'. She and John were glad to become known by the name of their new home, because they were very happy together, and the Faroese islanders were happy that a place that had been silenced by the Plague now rang again with laughter. The Princess of Suðuroy and John Sinclair prospered, and soon they had a small son. The only thing that spoiled their happiness was the thought that one day King James might find them.

Sure enough, one summer they saw a large fleet of ships on the horizon. As it sailed nearer and nearer, the Princess of Suðuroy ran to find her husband John Sinclair. "Quick," she said to him, "run and hide up in the outfield." John Sinclair did not want to hide, but the Princess of Suðuroy was afraid of what her father would do, and she made her husband promise to go where he might be safe. Then the Princess lifted up her son and carried him down to the shore. Her son was still a very small boy, and he knew that something was wrong and was afraid, and clung to his mother and wanted milk. So when King James' boat arrived at the shore he found his daughter sitting at the shoreline, nursing her son. And even though King James had set out from Scotland with anger in his heart, as soon as he saw his daughter like this, and saw his own grandson, all his anger melted away.

As King James walked towards the Princess of Suðuroy, his grandson looked up, and, when King James started to speak, the little boy reached out his hands, unafraid, to try and touch the bright gold chain that King James wore around his neck. King James, the Gudeman of Ballengeich, took his grandson into his arms, and let him play with the chain, and he looked at his daughter. There were many things that could have been said, about the Princess' mother, and about how people could have behaved differently, but in that moment of silence between the adults the child chuckled. Then those things remained unsaid, and they were reconciled. Behind the King, the men of the Clan Gunn, who had sailed with him from Scotland, stood happy, pleased that the Princess of Suðuroy and John Sinclair were safe.

King James and the men of Clan Gunn stayed with the Princess of Suðuroy and John Sinclair for a few days. Each day, King James and his grandson played together by the shore. On the last day, King James asked the Princess of Suðuroy and John Sinclair to return with him and the Clan Gunn to Scotland, but they declined, and said that they would like to stay in the Faroe Islands, where they were happy. And so the King and the men of Clan Gunn sailed home, and the Princess of Suðuroy and John Sinclair lived for the rest of their lives in the Faroes, where they had more sons, and daughters, and more people came to stay near them, until there was a small settlement there.

And that was almost the end of the story. But the Clan Gunn were not happy: John Sinclair had been fostered with them to try and help end the enmity between the Clan Gunn and the Sinclairs. The fights between the Gunns and the Sinclairs had been long and bitter, and now that John Sinclair was gone the Gunns felt that their clan had been weakened. King James did not see at first how he could fix this, but then he remembered that the Clan Gunn had always had strong links with others, with people who were non-Scots. Some people said that the Clan Gunn were Picts, and some said that they were Vikings, maybe Scandinavians who already had links with the Faroe Islands – and maybe that was why the Princess of Suðuroy was so happy in these northern isles. So King James suggested that the Clan Gunn form an alliance with the Faroese, and that, since John Sinclair had gone to the Faroe Islands, someone from the Faroe Islands should come to Scotland. And the Faroese agreed to this idea, as it seemed to them that they had much in common with the Scots, and that another link with them could well be a good thing. So from among their islands a young woman called Jofrid was chosen to travel to Scotland. And this now is the story of Jofrid, who became Jofrid Gunn.

The Skjaldur of the Violin of Jofrid's Wedding

On the wedding day of Jofrid
the Gunn man brought the fiddle
I took it in both hands
but the tune was trapped inside
I asked the wind to teach me
I asked the sea to guide me
the salt gave me its secret
but asked for an exchange.
Both my hands were full of stones
my head was full of sound
I wait for the boat of sailors
to return to the song they left me.

An echo is the language of the mountains

The low strong light paints the sea into a dreamscape
into a half-remembered echo of a night thought
told quietly in the language of the mountains

a broken egg-shell nestled in the grass of the cliff-top
is covered in shattered dark markings
unreadable now, this hidden language of the world

a straight line of guillemots
flies just above the surface of the sea
single birds dive fast, at an angle
the curve of the wing-beat the up-and-down of letter-strokes

the loss of a secret runic alphabet
that only the huldufólk could understand
scribing territorial intent: these cliffs, these stacks,
this single pear-shaped egg is mine

watching at a distance, apart from the abundant, gregarious birds
the light fades and the huldufólk come into their own
we need to learn to love the darkness again
to enter into their world, learn their language once more

The Dancing in the Hall

If you want to hear my story
The faithful truth of it,
The story of Jofrid Gunn
We begin here:

From the outside
I hear the dancing
In the hall
The footsteps resounding

The worry had started earlier
Come the morning
Come the danger
Come the boy who wants to be the warrior

The dance beats in a ring
Circle resounding
Sing – here are the north-men
Sing – here are my clan

I was not born here but
I was married here
Now the fear-dream
That takes over:

Here comes my man to the hall
I will not stand beside him
His strong hand
Raised against my family

I am named Jofrid Gunn
My choice of name brings tension
Father's daughter
Loyalty in person

They swarm from the hall
Down to the sea's edge
Follow and raise the standard
Drive it into the brown earth

The shouting echoes out and on
Drifting back along the sea road
The haar comes in with loneliness,
stillness and the silence

Everyone hears the thunder
The crash of plans ruining
What place is there for a wife here
Whose kinsmen fight her husband

The weather twists my prayers
The ship is broken before me
The men are back without fighting
Death, without blood-feud

Now this story cannot end here
I cannot say goodbye here
There is a long time of living after
Long recriminations.

Outside

winter has taken the colour out of everything
the grass is yellow, sparsely raked over the mud
by the constant wind
the sky cleared
scudding ragged clouds away
and cold.
It's too cold, really, to stay outside all night
the fire burns down and
the hot and black embers
shimmer the air directly around it
but the heat doesn't reach further out
doesn't warm deep to the bone.

Angles

At night when I am alone
I think of my husband in angles
the line of his cheekbone when seen from the side
the curve of the tops of his arms when he holds me
his hair when it is longer
the hair of his beard, parts of him.
In the dark I look at parts of me
my own arm, the curves that are not like his
All of these pieces
inhabited by the shape of one mind
Glimpses in the half-light twilight
Glimpses without words
His skin, pale. Mine, paler
the shadow around his eye
along his cheekbone
his hair swept off his face.

Silvertongue

There is the ghost of a language in my mouth
somewhere under a heavy silver tongue
a speaking voice full of thorns
the words crowd to get out
the throat closes, swallows,
all is yearning, yarning
I speak like an unloved child learning
groping back to half-remembered
beginnings, repeated phrases
the unfamiliar shapes of letters
the poets, adder-tongues,
can turn words into magic
I can barely turn them into facts
they say good poetry survives translation
bad poetry shrinks to nothing
I cannot translate myself
I am on the other side of a wall, catching
only snatches of laughter and warmth
whispers of love and family
the ghost of a language unshaped
a tongue too big for my mouth

Wedding ring shawl: advice from a mother-in-law

Make sure your tension is just right –
use Knitting Pins No. 6.
The pattern has been passed down from mother to daughter
for generations in our family –
cast on 175 stitches
it should be easy if you only follow my instructions –
knit in garter stitch for 175 rows
yes one hundred and seventy-five
the numbers are large but you should use
only Real Shetland Wool in purest, cleanest white
2 ply. The finest delicate strands of yarn.
Stretch the central square. We do the borders next.
Cast on 199 stitches.
This is the pattern and you must pay attention:
k1 * k2tog x3 m1 k1 alt x5 m1 k2tog x 3 k1
knit one (and here a star) knit two together times three make one knit one alternate times five make one knit two together times three knit one repeat.
And repeat the next part.
And soon your mind shall wander
knit one knit two together knit three together knit two together make one knit one alternate four times make one knit two together times three knit two together times three make one knit one alternate times five make one knit two together times three knit one repeat
until 18 remain
I may have left out some steps –
I've been doing this so long my hands have their own memory
you should now have reached
the 45th row.
You can walk and knit when you get the hang of it
your hands never rest
next 5 rows – knit
the wool is so fine that the best shawls,
the ones knitted by the best,

will slip through the centre of a wedding ring
these Ring Shawls are the finest they can be
57th row
I've only known two ring shawls: one was a wedding gift to me
from my own mother
and the other I made myself –
you can aspire to this.
63rd row: k2 ktog m1 k1 m1 k2tog k1 k2tog x 3
yes I missed a repeat
you should be able to see the errors yourself
by the 63rd row
no shawl is perfect
for nothing is perfect except what God makes.
I sometimes have to put an error in, on purpose.
Add an extra stitch
next 5 rows – knit. Cast off.
Make 3 more pieces in the same way.
When you make an error, you can rip back to it
place a marking thread
a needle – pin
whatever. It is difficult. But worth it, to remake things better.
Cast on 5 stitches for the edging.
Follow these instructions for 24 more rows –
repeat these 24 rows until sufficient is worked
to go round the entire shawl.
Cast off.
Then there is the pinning
and the pressing
and the sewing
and the pressing
you will get the hang of it eventually
and by the time you make your third child,
and your third blanket,
it will all come easier.

I dream about your death

I dream about your death.
I dream about the clothes
I would wear if you died
the words I would say if you died
how free I would be if you died –
the widow is the lucky woman:
free of her childhood home
free of her husband's home –

I dream about your death –
these thoughts bubble up like poison
bursting their way to near the surface
trying to force their way out
spill their secret over the edge
I hate you when I wake up
and you are still here –

I hate myself for these
wicked thoughts of death and freedom
there must be other routes to freedom –
I hold myself under control constantly
a watched and seething pot of boiling matter
I want to dream a different thing
but I cannot see it yet.

Uncontainable

One side of the hill lit up in the sunlight
the shadow moving like a line
pulled gently across the landscape
by the tugging clouds above

So much light, uncontainable
spilling down the cliffs and into the foaming sea
so much life crammed into one vision
the edge of the island is all that holds us together

The Song

The wind blows until my soul is tired.
Nothing is ever still – every hair is out of place –
across my eyes until I can no longer see
always dragging it away with my hands
until the brittle ends are snapping
like the ends of a flag tearing into strips
by the wind always constantly blowing.
On the hillside, it is too steep to imagine
the rock goes sheer down to the sea
the sky is like a wide mouth shrieking open
but someone has built a small grey stone wall to shelter
from the constant wind, and we stop here for a moment
stop from all the tasks. Try to cease. And you sing –
and it is an old song, I know some of the words
but not all. I could join in the chorus, but I don't, and
I'm not embarrassed to be watched watching you.
Unashamed
you perform and your voice
is deep and it anchors me to
the stones that form the shelter all around us,
the stones that come from the ground
and our roots and
and the wind and the song bring tears to my eyes
and it is perfect and I have never loved anyone
or any place as much as I love this fiercely right now
and even the wind is bearable,
even when it is so strong it blows the tears away
even before they form
even when it blows the song
until it scatters away over the hillside
but we met in the words
and I took the song, and kept the moment.

It happened so long ago it's not true anymore

It happened so long ago it's not true anymore
but the sheep are still in the field.
Thirsty with nostalgia, we pick up the thread
a twisted strand of soft grey wool following the yarn
as it knits into an old pattern of stars
the constellations a boat sailed by
the white wool of the starlight
the dark of the night sky
the grey of the dawn
and then a faded light brown
as the sun slowly sullenly reveals
half-bitten grass

Sodden light

cloud lies heavy – sodden light
wool dripping droplets hanging low over the field
wading forward into rain clouds
clothes darken moisture hangs in the air
walk into standing rain
soaking through to the skin

Sea Stacks

The giant stayed in the sea, while his wife the witch climbed the mountain, carrying a heavy rope. Together, they meant to lasso the island and tow it home to its sibling. The wife climbed in the darkness and rain, all through the night. The rope, looped over her shoulder, was heavy, and grew heavier as it got wet. From time to time she stopped, and changed the weight from one shoulder to the other. Then there was a momentary relief and the carrying grew easier, until the heaviness weighed on the new side and she had to stop again and repeat. She pushed on, feeling like she had passed her limit long ago, but determined on the task she had started. The cold pierced her skull.

When she reached the plateau, she attached the rope to the mountain, ready to pull. They would take the island home again, rejoin the mothers with their children, rejoin what never should have been broken apart. But when she finally got the rope around the jagged part of the mountain and began to pull, ready to bring it downwards to her husband the giant, the northern part of the mountain would not move. As she pulled harder, it still did not move forward, but only split, a great jagged tear that sliced close to the ground but did not shift the base. She cried and her tears mixed with the rain running down her face so that no one would notice. She tried again and again to encircle the island with the rope, dreaming of how, together, she and the giant could pull on the rope and tow it homewards. They would wade knee-deep through the sea, splashing in the surf.

Mighty and powerful, they would close the gap and the people standing on the headland would gasp as they saw the islands join together again. They would be pleased. But in the rain and the growing wind, the rope would not fit around the island, and the witch grew more and more tired. She could not see or hear her husband the giant over the noise of the surf and the waves and the constant battering against the coastline. She did not know if he helped or not. And slowly and gradually the dawn came and the night was ended, and she sat down and knew that the task was impossible. Out from the cliff edge now stood a new sea stack; the giant turned into stone as the sun hit him. As she watched, the stone turned a rosy warm pink and orange colour. It invited climbers. And the witch, exhausted, stood now as if she too were turned to stone, feeling as if the next round of winter storms would be her last, because it was not possible to be so far from home, so unable to join the two islands of her heart.

This is a Feigdarferð, doomed sea journey.

This is a journey where we don't reach home
the stones never tell you that you belong
the landscape will never gather round you
like a cloak, fitted for warmth, loved, well-used.

The uncaring mountain will shrug you off
each step will always stumble, tentative
every footprint leaves an accusing scar
a reminder that you should not be there.

What does it take to love with certainty
to belong to this place unthinkingly
give it only a glance as you stride through
 expect that it will rearrange round you.

Stay, sit outwith, beside the mountain by
the sea. Wait here a moment, wait with me.

A silent sunset

A silent sunset
Swelling clouds rising and pressing the sky
Orange weighted
Bridging the river

Out of Place

A traveller, out of place
he spoke of towns and streets with steps to shops
doors that opened straight to the world
the mountains did not hoard his soul, he was apart –

his skills were different: fixing and selling,
he brought news: a chain of information
collected on his travels; took news
back, binding us with others, a link

after the long winter,
when there was no more to say to your neighbour,
the travellers arrived just in time
to show us we were not alone here
life is always moving, always moving.

A lullaby for his daughter

My little daughter lullaby
My new fair nursing child
The light fades low so slowly
You grow heavy in my arms.

Slate-blue eyes blink open
Short lashes show a glance
The night world knows our watching
Our nonsense lullabies.

I sing songs of a smaller island
Of birds and journeys, boats and families
Keep going in colour and in weather
To the house near cliffs like home.

I'll sing in the language I've learned here
In the new words of this north
I hold you my girl, his daughter,
sleep now, my new fair nursing child.

Sólja

he sits in stillness
his back to the house
a focus
birds dipping
like small brown heavinesses
through the air around him.
the small yellow flowers on the grass
are sólja – buttercup
the wind drops, pausing before
it starts rifling through the petals again
tiny white flowers grow,
no longer than short green grass blades,
at the top of the windblown mountains
in the Faroes
snow buttercup
snjósólja
tiny purple flowers in the moss here
circle flower
weed spread
out of place
I envy his thoughtful contemplation
he looks like a man creating –
if only poems came from stillness.

Juniper

The baby is quiet
with a teething twig of juniper

more twigs burn in the hearth
stealthily, with little smoke

the wood protects us
keeps the night at bay

we withstand the cold, the snow,
the wind outside, the blaze itself

regenerating, our heartwood glowing
pink and brown, protected by the red bark

drink: throat-fire, gin-fire, warm
against the cold. The stew pot,

venison, so slowly on the fire.
Like child's hands clinging around the neck

shrubs cling to the hillside
growing inch by inch over the dark peat ground

the Clan Gunn badge: Juniper
the mountain yew, sharp blue-green needled

secure by the heather on the moor
under the pine and birch

birds fly south from Scandinavia
for its black berries: field fare.

The baby is quiet
with a teething twig of juniper

we are cocooned from harm
in our family's home in winter.

The Hammerbeam Roof
at Darnaway Castle, Moray

We travelled through the firthlands by ferry
under blue-grey clouds that filled the sky and
smirred the edge of the land in mist and rain

in the meeting hall a thousand men could
stand together, shoulder to armed shoulder
under the vast high oak hammerbeam roof

the timbers darkened from the fire's smoke
the wood ancient, cut from trees that have seen
what men have forgotten, other times past

the secret carvings high in the rafters
watch us: bear eyes, wolf eyes, ornate faces
the weight resting on craftsmen's wide shoulders

the wood swells as I watch through the noise
the roar of men talking rising upwards
til the air catches the sea's buoyancy

the timbers shape like the sides of a boat
the hall steering us through the ocean, neat
coils of rope by bracing curving posts

outside, gables like dark sails take us back
to the firths, then leave ferries far behind
chasing those looming clouds, outrun rain.

The Parting Hymn

The wind was keening in the night
a low whistle rising and falling into a moan
this morning there are still squalls – it blusters,
promising storms but raising nothing.

The boats make ready to go out.
The wood creaks, timbers shifting,
the water slapping against the sides of the boats
arrhythmic, catching every time
angling its way, insidious

in the cold of early half-light
where sleep subdues noise
the hymns begin quietly.
Each boat has its own song
to start the fishing day
the verse and chorus
of an outdoor church
the entanglement of voices
reaching up to the sky

What makes the churches fall silent –
the plague, the bells unrung
the people afraid to gather together.
But here, in the unceasing search for food
– wooden pillars of masts
would reach up to crosstrees –
smaller rowed boats. Families:
brothers and fathers and uncles and sons

oarsmen pull together the prayer heard sung
the parting music for safe return.

A Riotous Serious Garden

My children have each planted a garden. My eldest son has a serious garden; practical vegetables grow in rows, ripening ready to eat one after another in rotation. He measures and waits for harvest, then shares, delighted to see us eat what he has grown. He believes it tastes better than anything he has ever eaten elsewhere. My youngest son has a riotous garden: berry-bushes, chosen for their flowers, and growing in a tangle. He grew bored after planting and has no idea when the fruit will be ready, until his brother reminds him. Then he comes and eats berry after berry until his laughing lips are staining red, and when his brother asks why he didn't share he just shakes his head and says, well why didn't you just take some? Their father watches them and says to me that the gardens were meant to teach them how to take care, and he is not sure if they have both learnt the lesson. But I know better, because they are both my sons and I love them, but I know that however hard we try to teach them, one lives one way and one lives another. They are like two halves of a conflicting personality that wants to be in one place and also wants to be in another – and that is me, of course, their mother – but they are also their own personalities, and, although I tended them and tried to have patience, they came the way they were born and I just had to let them grow, in a tangle like the berry-bushes. I can't shape them but I gave them what I have which is love. And both their gardens have colour and love but most importantly they are side-by-side and the berries fall into the eldest's garden and he watches the youngest's garden and that is not a perfect way to be, but it is a way – and both gardens, alongside, are alive and bursting with fruit.

Moss

My fingertips scrabble in the moss
the soft grey-green, the glowing reds
the moisture caught at the roots
the dark earth caught under my white nails
the bright-green turf surrounding us
like a sprung dancefloor strewn with field flowers
brushed by the constant music of the wind
inviting bare feet
pushing us to join a wild dance

a poem like the curves of the stone

a poem like the curves of the stone
the carvings of circles, knotwork interlaced
the ink blue under the skin
a skin poem, sailor's tattoo
an arrow leading home, an anchor tethering the soul

The Mother Troll

Life with the children was sometimes good, but sometimes the troll came in from the field outside. When the troll came in, everything went wrong. Towards the evening, the troll would sit in the middle of the room, with his hat turned inside out, wearing his jacket with the seven pockets, and slowly brushing his grey fur. As he brushed his grey fur, small hairs came loose and fell down to the ground below him. Only those with the gift of magic could see him of course, but he affected everyone. Jofrid was arranging the evening meal. She could not see the troll, but soon enough she became aware that something was not right. There was not enough room for the children to play when the troll was squatting in the middle of the room. The children began to fall over each other, pushing and shoving and squabbling. Jofrid had to leave the food and come to pull them apart. She sent each child to sit in a different corner of the room, but the children got scared and anxious when they had to sit apart, as all they could each see was the troll, sitting impassively in the middle. So the children ran through to where Jofrid was preparing the table, getting under her feet and clinging onto her. The food preparation became more difficult, and Jofrid became angry with the children. Then the children crept back to the room where the troll still sat combing his grey fur. As the small hairs and clumps of fur fell onto the floor, the troll carefully bent down and picked them up, and put them into one of his seven pockets. But, however careful the troll was, some of the hairs floated away. When they landed on the children, the hairs irritated them, until they felt uncomfortable in their own skin. Dinner was late, as Jofrid had had such trouble arranging the meal, and after they had eaten, the children did not feel full and rested. At night, the troll's hair still irritated them, and they could not lie still in their beds. They did not sleep through the night, and Jofrid had to get up to soothe them several times. In the morning, everyone felt dull and heavy. Jofrid sent the children outside, and the fresh air blew away many of the troll's irritating grey hairs, but in the evening the troll came back again, and sat in the middle of the room again, wearing his battered hat turned inside out, his jacket with the seven pockets, and slowly brushing his grey fur. The second evening was when Jofrid truly began to suspect the troll's presence. The following morning, after another night of disturbed sleep, Jofrid left the house in a state of disarray, and went outside with her children. A fresh breeze was blowing, and straight away it helped to blow the stray hairs from the grey troll away from them. Jofrid walked with the children until they came to the edge of the field, where a large boulder sat. Jofrid knew, because her own mother had told her, that this would be the home of the troll. She gathered the children around her, and they played there for hours, shouting and laughing and enjoying themselves. The children loved spending time with their mother. Meanwhile, the troll, who was trying to sleep under the rock, got no rest at all. That evening, instead of coming down to sit in the house, the troll was still sleeping. The children did not squabble, they had their meal in peace, and that evening Jofrid and her family all slept well. For all the rest of that week, Jofrid took her children up to the troll's rock, and they played and shouted and laughed there. By the end of the week, the troll's habit had been broken, and that evening he turned his hat the right way round and walked away in the opposite direction, away from Jofrid's house.

Other Mothers

My arms are angles,
lines that change abruptly,
sharp elbows,
unnatural.
Other mothers embrace,
their children rest their soft heads, secure.
So many things I can't do as a mother:
spiders, mice.
Across the wooden floorboards I walk
angry and awkward, bare feet cross and cold
to pick them up.
Other cheerful mothers scoop up children one-handed
with love, automatic, unthinking
a natural part of their life, their curved figure –
meanwhile my thoughts run
backwards and forwards,
checked and rechecked
I am only pregnant with words
a surfeit of words
I don't love them less
I can nurse the sick child
I love them fierce but
through that angular barrier,
at a distance
I want to gather them into
a Madonna and child circle
containing nothing but
the milk and the love
but instead I have the words in there too
the observation and the learning and the rethinking
and the awkwardness and strange angles.

the wood is pathless…

the wood is pathless, each track an animal's
secret route, not a trail to follow
I walk like a mapless townsman,
a shore dweller, not used to holding the line
there are wolves, they are still here.
I imagine their howls.
I think of the walk as a fight with the forest
a thing to get through, a line that must be drawn:
you wander, stop to examine trees
stoop to pick berries,
leave even what passes for a path.
with no horizon, I can't imagine where the sea is
you are unconcerned,
follow a small indentation in the ground
as if it is a real place to walk,
imagine that you will come out somewhere
and then figure out how to walk back
to where you know.
I am tired. I do not want to explore.
I need to finish this task, return home,
because there are so many more.

The Geese flew in a V-shape overhead

I don't know where the birds fly to
– I probably should – every year
you see them, the V overhead.
They return, the weather changes.
I think – there's an open sky – when is it?
I remember blue and cold.
The noise draws me to the door.
I look up, think of journeys,
seasons going, people not returning.
Back in the shadows of the house
I glimpse you dressing
think of the patch of skin
at the base of your throat,
the open collar of your shirt untied,
making a V of flesh.
I think of being
– not a child, a teenager,
and my mother would stand on the doorstep
and say, look, the geese,
and we did not understand
why it was interesting
because, of course,
they returned every year,
it was a thing we had seen
I never asked the questions then
of where do they fly to
– where do they fly from –
and how do they know.

an impossible island

sometimes
the memories of childhood
seem impossible
an incessant island
with sides so steep
we had to cling to them,
fingers digging into the earth
a deep cold, a howling wind,
the grey trolls –
and set against that:
the warmth of family
a unit long gone,
dissolved in dreams
a lost thing –
yet it all resurfaces
all-encompassing
in a passing taste
and smell of smoke
from the fire,
the smoke filling
the whole hall,
the whole lungs
a sensation that lurches
more than the mind,
the whole body
until it must be taken out
into the clear night air
– but to find there
in the quiet darkness still
a gathering,
puckering of memory
the touch of a hand
the feel on skin
of the impossible past.

Breathing

down by the shore,
the sea is breathing in and out
in gentle wavelets, the sky is calm,
bigger than my eyes can hold,
but the clouds are closing in –
there is weather in the sky
behind the hill.

When the rain comes,
the water becomes a wall
I can no longer imagine crossing
the lurch, the pitch and yaw of the boat.
Holding flat to the deck,
the spray coming over, the sea
with no edges like the sky,
a malicious salt thing that tangles
into hair and eyes and clothes and limbs.

When they pray to the sea to listen,
I think of the fear that
it might not hear what we ask of it,
that it might choose not
to give up its secrets, its bodies,
but greater fear is the thought of no care:
no intercession, no gods,
only the wall of blue grey white,
the green dark ocean. The weather,
just coming,
the sea,
not breathing.

The memorial stone stands

The memorial stone stands
like a big man with his arms folded
strong shoulders set,
back to the land and
facing out to sea.
The waves are summer light
gentle folds on the shore
the depths of the storm hidden
in the stone on the shore.

Stops

When the noise stops

when the children halt screaming
and the washing rests banging
and the wind breaks off howling
and the birds end yammering
and the rain is soft on the earth –
the internal clamour begins.

the shadow and promise of noise lingers, impedes,
the quiet discontinued,
the wants unceasing
the others', and also:
a craving for something
something that needs silence first,
to be described.

Look at the dirk he wears, from Caithness
handmade by the local blacksmith to wear
at the county fair
with foreknowledge of the bloodshed
often seen at that rough affair
longer than a Highland dirk.
A cross between that and a Norwegian knife,
with its long, narrow blade.
The sheath covers the dirk
halfway up the handle.
A cross between two cultures.

Now. Take the knife in your imagination:
the sharpness can pare down to a point
it is a tool and not a weapon
this is not an argument,
it is a route I need to find –

scrape out a gentle hollow in the mind
a place that can always hold silence
a place of mine
then

sit the words there –
the secret images.
The stories,
the islands of thought
move the noise into patterns.

Control where it begins and ends.

Up and down

We walk up to the village
and down to the sea.
A lot of people have a dial –
Set me down, spinning
Like a compass
And I'll turn north
and further north
Back up
To home
In the clear night sky
the constellations star the way
And the shadow pointing
from the midday sun.

The Clan Gunn's Stories

The Clan Gunn were divided among the three countries of Sutherland, Caithness and Strathnaver. The Gunns lived to the south of the lands of the Sinclair Earls of Caithness, and to the north of the lands of the Gordon Earls of Sutherland, and sometimes crossed over into the Mackay clan lands of Strathnaver. That is to say, the Gunns were on the border, in the middle of three enemies; the bridge and the barrier.

"Sinclair, Sutherland, Mackay, and Clan Gunn; Never was peace where those four were in…" At one time, the Gunns found the Sinclairs more in tune with their ideals as a clan. Although the Sinclairs were Earls and swore allegiance to the crown, they were also strongly linked by blood and marriage to the Clan Mackay in the Far North. Through their allegiance with the Mackays, the Sinclairs understood and respected how the clan system worked. One of the Sinclair sons was even fostered with the Gunns: nourished and brought up in his infancy within the clan. However, over time, things became complicated. It became a time full of trouble and discord.

The tipping point came when the Clan Mackay changed allegiance. The Clan Mackay stopped supporting the Sinclairs and began to run with the Gordons of Sutherland. As the position of their neighbours on either side changed, so the Clan Gunn became nervous. The Gordons grew in stature even as the Sinclairs were cast down and, as the Gordons grew more powerful, they grew more disdainful of the clans around them. The Gordon allegiances stretched far, up to the north and the Orkney islands, and down to the powerbases and royal seats in Stirling and Edinburgh. The Gordons found the Clan Gunn troublesome, and laid deep plans to get rid of them.

As the Clan Gunn were nervous, when they heard that many men were mobilising around the area where they lived and that a group was on the march driving cattle before them, the men of the Clan Gunn too began to arm themselves and gather together. This became known as the fateful day of Claw-tom-richi, or The Day of the Heather Bush. The men of Clan Gunn took themselves to the top of the heather-covered hill, and soon saw the Clan Mackay arriving. The Mackays had been raiding cattle, but had had the misfortune to run into a marching army of Gordons. These Gordons had set out on a march towards the Sinclair territory, but they were not so set on their plan that they did not want to defend their cattle, and they turned on the Mackays, despite the alliance that meant the Mackays were supposed to be their friends.

Now, the Gunns found that the Mackays were on one side of them and the Sinclairs on another, and the Gordons were coming up close on a third, and no one had any idea anymore who supported who. The Mackays reached the heather-covered hill first, hailing the Gunns as friends. They hastily persuaded the Gunns to unite with them. The clans, said the Mackays, should stay together in the face of the earls. Look how the Gordons could turn on the Mackays, they said. Clans and earls should not mix. The Clan Gunn swithered, but the Sinclairs arrived next.

These, now, are our enemies, said the Mackays. The Clan Gunn made their choice, and chose to hazard against the Sinclairs. They did this without fear or delay, despite being far inferior in number – the Gunns were always courageous, though that courage was sometimes said to come from desperation. There was nothing before the Gunns but enemies, and nothing behind them but the deep and bottomless ocean. There was no place of retreat and no way out but through valour and victory.

The Clan Gunn had the advantage of height, being placed high on that hilltop amongst those ankle-high heather bushes, and they stood tight as the Sinclairs began to advance. The Sinclairs shot their first flight of arrows, but the Clan Gunn spared their shot until the enemy was hard upon them; and only then loosed their arrows, to great advantage. The light began to fail and the Sinclair men took flight, running home to Caithness. The darkness prevented the Clan Gunn from following, as it prevented the Gordons from arriving.

But it was not to be expected that the Sinclairs would forget the defeat. Afterwards, they pursued Clan Gunn with great ferocity. The Gunns' alliance with the Mackays, formed so hastily on the heather-topped hill, was a hollow friendship. The Mackays, now allied decisively with the Gordon Sutherlands, supported the Gordons above all others and then the real harm came, for the cunning and clever Gordons gradually worked until the north was all theirs and they held the real power. They took the Mackays with them, and they tricked the Sinclairs into following them, and they gradually united them all in opposition to the Gunns.

After much fighting, many of the men of Clan Gunn did not come home, and some of those that did come home decided that they must pack up their bags and go to somewhere safer. Men and women of the Clan Gunn took the roof beams of their houses on their backs and walked, in a single, straggling line through the mist and over the hills, to new homes where they hoped they would be safe.

Some of the Clan Gunn did stay, and sometimes they were briefly friends with the Sinclairs, and sometimes with the Gordons and the Mackays, but mostly they did what they could on their own. But one of the saddest things was that their stories began to slip away. With so few members of the clan to gather now, there were fewer and fewer people to listen to the stories, and fewer and fewer storytellers to pass them on. They began to be a clan without their own stories, whose stories were lost. Soon enough they began to believe the stories that others told about them.

The others' stories said that Clan Gunn was different to the rest; that they had not come from the north, but had come from the Vikings; from Gun, the younger son of the King of Denmark. Perhaps, they whispered, they had even come from the earlier folk, the Hidden Folk. Perhaps they did not belong in the north at all. The Clan Gunn no longer knew what was true or not, but they made their disappearing origins into a badge of honour: we are different, they said, we are not like you Sinclairs or you Gordons or you Mackays. And sometimes that was a good thing, because they could say to the Gordons and Mackays, no, of course we would never stand with the Sinclairs against you. We are not like the Sinclairs. And sometimes it was a bad thing, because the Gordons and Mackays would say to the Sinclairs, who are the Clan Gunn? They are not like us, we should join together and get rid of them.

But the worst thing for a clan is to lose its stories. Sometimes it doesn't even matter what the stories are, or whether or not they are true, the important thing is just that someone is telling them. The clan comes into being through its stories. It almost does not exist in real life if it does not exist in the imagination first. So the Clan Gunn searched for a storyteller, and took what they could. They took other people's stories, and other people's music, and the stories from other places, and built them into something new, and they hung on, a bridge and a barrier, a clan on their own.

The Burial Party

We go to the sea,
to the earth,
a true feigdarferð this time,
a journey with no return
through land or sea or air
a gravarferð, grave voyage
the earth-going
talk around it three times in a circle
this mourning for a son.

Dream of the bodies
coming home in the darkness
the oars slipping into the water
away from foreign lands,
fetch the men home by boat
pulling through the ocean
with the coffins on board
singing a hymn
and then as dawn comes,
they row three times
sunwise in a circle, still singing,
then proceed on their way,
never landing.

In the morning, there is no body to bury
the children, young men, lie abroad
souls slipped away
no lair in the kirkyard,
they dwindle from the hope of return
to a mother's memory
no last comfort, last touch
just the distance
of the immense salt
of the sea between us –

so the women walk
three times around the church,
still singing

to try to bring the rest.

Unmoored

I feel lost – adrift, unmoored
a small brown wooden boat
paint peeling
no oars or anchor
bobbing just out from the shore
under a wide light blue sky
if you wade out it is
just an arm's-grasp away
four steps out of your depth
the cold water slaps
small tendrils of unrealised power

shore-dweller

Song of a shore-dweller
not an ocean-goer
not a sailor, not a rower
no palm blisters
swelling fingers
a shoreline woman
in the house with children
shrugged off the sealskin
stepped up from the sea
I know the sea, I hate the ships
I love the ships, I hate the sea
I'm in my place
beside it here

Creagh-Drumi-Doun

The actions of the *Sluagh*, the host,
the people of the clan –
their asperous names –

Creagh the raid
plundering
the first foray in the Far North
Drumi the drums beating
the new Mackay clan chief nervous
doun go down
running
the hill towards the enemy

the noise of it:
the drums
      beating, beating
the arrows loosed,
      breaking the air, then
the wind rushing
      on the run downwards
the feet tearing
      through the stiff roots, rough and bleeding
the grunt
      of bodies meeting
the clash,
      the wet slither of blade into flesh
the crunch that bones make
      breaking into the wooden targe edge

the silence of it:
the blood roaring deafening
heart sound trapped in the ears
a shout half-stifled
the drums slowly beating, beating, stopping

the speed of it,
a fight,
the incongruous birds
startled into the sky,
their flight spins
lazily back down
curious
the drip of a small
stream of water
pooling in the heather
by the blood
the tang of the air

back at the top of the hill
a drummer
picking up his drum
picking his way slowly, carefully
through the heather that cut feet
on the charge
that heartbeat beating

others
gathering
after the stumble home

the fierceness of the raid:
the Mackay splinter
    rushing on the clan Gunn
in revenge for their dependence
their rents paid to Sutherland,

the young chief riding right through
the carefully nurtured alliance
of Mackay and Gunn,

leading Sutherland to
invade the Mackay lands:

the great prey of goods
the spoil, the waste
the long,
the many horrible encounters
the bloodshed,
the infinite spoils
    of disordered and
    troublesome memory

the confusion of places,
    times and persons
    is war to the reader

the meaning fades out of the argument,
    only the hurt and the name remain
the sound of the drum, the heart beat,
the running downhill:
    Creagh-Drumi-Doun.

Ancestors

Who cares what our ancestors did?
their stunted lives, full of error
rutted old ways, lacking knowledge
Tread down the ancestors now
Pull walking feet from the cloying earth
Move forward, cut free
from the dead weight branches
to the light
Move to the new insistent drumbeat
technical and fast and clear and sweet.

Intent, discourage, follow, falter

a decade too late, or a day too late
the life you wanted is already gone

late to the party, chasing a memory
the conversation has turned and moved on

the table is bare, the seats overturned –
a half-remembered route you once started –

now an ending –
now an unwanted ending has faltered

an idea, an intent discouraged

the book that you read, the people to meet
the dream that you followed seems finished and done

a seat pulled back, a glass sits half-empty
the night is falling, the twilight is long

that half-remembered route you intended
a path once started now ends in the dark

the trees in the wind make shapes in the night
but pause, stop, for this ending has faltered

stop: here on the ground: a new mark
here on the ground are new footsteps, a mark

a new start –
a start, a child, who walks on their own

a glimpse of a future, something not gone
a glimpse of a future to follow this poem.

Froth

Take the glass
– blow the froth from the top to make
the bubbles blind the witches' eyes –
and settle the darkness.
Stars dance in the sky
the moon hangs large
and is content.
The sea today was calm,
fishing was contemplation.
Wife and waiting cheerful children.
The waves brought the boats gently ashore
the land welcomed us
the world loved us home.

The Votive Ship

The sea-water is clearer than you thought – not blue
but the ship lies deep as you dive down through
opaque shimmer, the dark green kelp shivers
drowned forest parting as the current shows the wreck.
Lying on its side, the water moves through
every space in it, seeping between boards
pulsing the swollen wood slowly outwards
inside is dark and you move away, do not look.
Turning with the drift, instead glancing up
the kelp seaweed meets overhead like an
underwater cathedral but the weight
of the water pushes cold and dark and
endless and there is no direct way to the sky
and you take a breath and your eyes open
only the saltwater of tears remains
on your eyelids and blink up into the
cavern of god's own cathedral filled with
only air, the lightness, song soaring round
you and in your arms the votive ship.

Your offering, to god, if he is listening,
and to the sea in your pleading
each miniature plank of wood
carved like the original.
Holding in its frame
the love and the loss, the fear
of the forgotten deep below,
your dream, to guide them from
the wreck.

There are many things in the sea
that don't exist.

The Original Jofrid

Outside in the dawn is the diamond sound:
the hush of wind sends thin slices of cold
through the canvas but somewhere
water is dripping; thawed:
the sun is warming the moving grass
and the piercing oystercatchers call:
the sound of the possibility of clear sky
and spring.

Jofrid stands in the middle of the saga:
a disruption. Her tent pitched
by the side of the slope leading up to the shieling
the grass still pale and not yet recovered in green,
and she becomes the line that must be followed as
the winter of tales is over. This is a new story.

The shelter huts where the animals graze
on the mountain in summer:
they move – transhumance –
from their winter home
in the slow move of the seasons,
the animals stumbling, bunching
together then moving apart in the open,
as Jofrid leaves the fine homestead
of her father and mother in search
of adventure. Her sister is already elsewhere.

This is the original Jofrid's story:
from the half-open tent door, she can see
her father Gunnar: black shoes, long cloak
as he strides towards the animals on the hillside –
far more real than the grey shadows of men
who move alongside with their beasts
to the pasture: the hidden folk.

In the days spent alone there,
Jofrid spoke to the Huldufólk
who told her she would marry twice,
lose many times but gain so much:
a daughter, they said, so fair that poets
lost their hearts and words to her.
Jofrid listened to their warnings
but stood alone: a diamond.
Disruptive.

Jofrid Gunn thought that
her name had marked her.
Sometimes, she felt that
the key to her life could be found
in her namesake's story: but
which share of that story
was the more important?
the threads of the original Jofrid's life
ran through more than one saga:
she pitched on similarities.

'I had rather', said Jofrid,
'that no trouble should arise
because of me' –
that most remarkable lady –
travellers stopped in time by her tent
for a kind greeting, and she was well pleased
with the match. She knew in the end
that troubles always follow:

the grace is in the dealing.

Robert Gordon and the burning of the papers of the Earl of Caithness

The riders gathered, restless in the grey early
dawn, the horses shifting, shadows of movement the
memory of kelpies, flanks wet with sweat or streaming water
at the end of a long ride out of the darkness
towards the stronghold and now awaiting orders.

A magical rider, bursting forth avenging from a family
myth clutching an order of fire and sword from the king
leading men against their enemy. Or an old rancour and
a man afraid to fight alone but backed up by his kin and
his crown and taking every step to make it safe –

dull armour does not catch the slowly rising
sun, the mist is still clinging wet and heavy and
the damp seeps into the bones of the men
and the animals and the land all around
half-hidden by light and smoke.

The fires started, they take hold slowly at first.
There is no one in the castle, the countryside was warned
of our arrival and there is nothing left but a chest full of papers
and he kneels in front of it, tearing through documents
a hasty glance but everything is committed to the fire

how can a true historian let it go so easily?
Does he know what he is burning –
the paper and parchment and vellum glows red at the heart
the wind is rising and lifting floating torn scraps of paper
whirl in the rising heat of the fire
up into the sky the systematic destruction
of a written history – what sort of fight is this?

against stories against legal papers
in the restless gathering dawn
there are no written documents, no stories in my island:
that does not mean we have forgotten.
The memories are there of the riders and the morning,
but we have no proof. No place to point,

say, it is there, on the page, only a memory
of a man on his knees reading, and burning,
the leaves scattering round his lawyer's heart,
the hard cold metal keys of the strong castle delivered
and resting on the grass beside him the riders restless,
only the morning advancing.

Pulse

Under the fragile skin of the earth
at the frayed edges of the coastline,
jagged by the eating sea
the bones scratch through to the surface

our thin soil barely covers the rock
the wind scours the stones wearing them away,
until the island itself will drown in the sea
heedless of the people clinging there

in the constant light of the summer
the rock gives a sudden small sparkle;
crystal, translucent with the light that passes through
the pulse that lies below the surface almost visible.

He wrote asking for a suit of scarlet and grey

They are to marry soon and I think I must be there
and seeing I have no clothes here
I have thought it good hereby
to request you to cause ask for one John Turner,
tailor in Edinburgh, who is son-in-law to George Kerr,
who was our old man, with whom I left
a suit of black figured silk and a taffeta cloak,
which I request you to cause get,
and send it to me with the boy
I sent with my last letters to you.
And fail not to send me another one,
much scarlet, or fine grey London cloth
with a base to line it, and silver lace and
buttons to sew it, conforming to the best
and newest fashion, as will be my riding coat
and send all with the boy I sent to you last
and whatever it costs you I shall deliver it
on your arrival here.

Bride

She will be a bread-feast bride,
marrying at Lammastide
Beginning fresh, a starting day
Church and harvest coincide
The tealzeour-tailor, cutter, sewer
Will cloak us all in finery
The siller, lace, the trim, the best,
And then an coitt for over all
An dochter tocherit, a daughter lost
Quhilk gained: a son-in-law,
a family, these future hopes, a happiness
This quarter-day, the bells, the noise, rejoice
The children scrambling round the church
This finery, emotion day
Her long gold hair unbound
The colour of the rippling fields of needed grain
The beginning of the harvest work
I feel a diffidence in speaking all
My memories – do all people's memories
change to sadness over time?
So I only say out loud
My August bride
My child, my girl
I am your mother here
At Lammastide.

A plea for understanding and remembrance: wishing to have disputes settled

To my very honourable good man and loving father, this:

I am only one and let never the earth bear me
but come nearer, hear my story and believe me:

It is no little grief to me to hear the reports –
I would be loathe to sit with such a wrong,
my service unrememberit –
and otherways remember, likewise
the world shall know
what travail, trouble and crosses were borne –

When on that day I came from the island
to this cold Far North and saw what would be my home
I was not careless of these particulars:
the obligation of duty and blood
the faith, trust and credit of all.

The wrong way it is to fall out is besetting me:
It is best that it settles in time, before we both repent too late
and leave our friends to lament our folly
I discharge my conscience to god and my duty to you.
Bind us in friendship.

An honest heart covers the smaller sins
and much can be forgiven.
So tell me that the tryst will hold,
or where it shall hold, or what day
and I shall rest and shall ever remain

Yours.

Boat Burning

I see the boat burning
the red of the flames and the smoke rising
hear the crackle of the wood
and a strong rhythm more like a heartbeat
than the irregular waves of the sea

the noise of stamping feet
the music for a wedding
a celebration, a loved boat leaving
my eyes are stinging tears from the smoke

the careful placing of the birds' large webbed feet
as they trample down at the edge of the cliff-side
the crushed shells on the sea-shore
there is no way to the sea now the boat is gone.

the travelling never stops

the travelling never stops.
the destination shifts and the
learned responses of the body change
travelling companions fall back, move forward
the steps are awkward
still, we face each new difficulty
holding, with ever more certainty
the endless circle, the decisive line
of the compass: north and always – true north.

The Violin

There were no musical instruments on the island until the year of Jofrid Gunn's wedding. One of the Gunn men had brought with him from Scotland a violin: the islanders had never seen such a thing before and crowded round when he began to play. Since they had never heard any fiddle player before the islanders might not have known whether he was good or not, but in fact he was an excellent musician. It was obvious to anyone that he made the music come alive. The fiddle danced and sung and spoke of things they had not known they wanted but now could not live without. Jofrid thought that it was maybe the violin that had reconciled her to the wedding: she thought that living in a place where she could hear music like that every day could only be magical. She knew little about the man she was to marry but the violin cast a spell. It brought people together and cast their thoughts in the same direction.

When Jofrid and the Gunn men were ready to leave and travel back to Scotland, the islanders begged that the violin should be left behind. One or two of the islanders had tried to play it; the fiddle player had shown them how to hold the bow and how to coax the notes out. Eventually, the violin player was persuaded: he was given a small part of Jofrid's dowry in exchange, and Jofrid left feeling that she had given her island a gift.

It was a strange gift, that needed a lot of work. Every evening, people gathered to try to make the violin sing. They knew how to hold the bow, and had watched the violin player closely, but it was hard to make the music themselves. The bow slipped and squeaked and the strings would not seem to hold the note. The violin player had warned them that the sea air was not good for the instrument so they took good care of it, but even still it seemed to lose its voice. They kept trying each night to practise; it was a good activity to pass the time as the winter drew in, but gradually there were fewer people still trying. It was easier to join in with the singing and chain dance that everyone knew how to do. One night there were only two boys there. One of them was trying to get the notes; he had managed to make the transition from one note to another smoother and smoother over time, and he played the same sequence again and again, his fingers getting more used to the action. He had no teacher to tell him that what he was doing was right or wrong, so he worked by ear, listening to the notes and matching them with what he knew from the songs. What he played was not like what the Scottish violinist had played, but it had a charm and a logic of its own. The other boy watched him, and at the same time was fashioning a carving, whittling some driftwood with a knife. It was a carving of the violin.

Occasionally, visitors and sailors from other lands would stop in the Faroe Islands. They were treated with caution – who knew how they would behave – but from time to time there was someone who knew about the violin, and then the boy would ask questions. If he was lucky, he would get useful answers, but he stored everything he learnt and tried as many techniques as he could to make the violin sing. He could not remember, now, exactly what the Gunn man had sounded like, but he tried to make his violin playing sound like the singing he heard around him, or like the sound of the wind on the hills, or the sound of the waves on the shore.

Time passed and the boy became the undisputed owner of the violin. He tried to show one or two people what he had taught himself, but they were mostly content to listen. When a visitor came to the island and listened along, he frowned and said it was like no violin that he had ever heard. But he listened quietly in the end. There was something about it, this self-taught violinist playing the sounds of an island without musical instruments.

The boy did not live long enough to marry and have children. He was drowned at sea; caught in a storm one spring. His mother put the violin carefully on the shelf to wait for another to play it, but the Gunn man had been right and the sea air did not agree with it. Something seemed to happen to the strings, or the wood – the islanders weren't quite sure, but the shape of the instrument became warped in some way. One night as the mother lay resting there was a sharp crack that startled her so much she thought her heart would stop beating. When she finally got the courage to investigate, she found that the noise had come from the violin, though she couldn't work out exactly how. But something in it was definitely broken and changed. Some of her neighbours said that the violin had broken itself in sorrow because its player was lost at sea. Soon, the violin became something that was only stored and forgotten, and some time after, when the mother had died, a distant relative, not knowing what it was, broke it up for firewood during that harsh winter when the snow lay for longer than it ever had and so many people were freezing.

There was only one reminder left of the Scottish violin. The boy who had watched his friend play, and had done the carving, remembered the shape of the violin. He became an expert craftsman, who many people asked for help when their houses were being built. A large beam of wood was washed up on the beach from a shipwreck, and this boy went down with the others to haul it up to the shore. It was when they were rebuilding the church, and the wood was put to good use. High up in the corner, where a beam was laid from side to side, that boy made a carving: a picture of the curves of the violin. He did it in memory of his friend, and of the strange music that he never heard again. The carving stayed there for almost two hundred years until the time when violins began to be imported to the islands regularly, and proper teachers showed the islanders how to make them play. Then, someone saw the carving and wondered if the violin had been heard and played on the islands before – and what it had sounded like, when there was only the sea and the wind to teach the violin player.

The Salt and the Coal

The salt on your skin
the salt in the air
the salt on your tongue
the sea crashing its waves on the shore nearby
the open earth up past the dunes nearby
the black coal heuchs shallow close to the surface
the earth giving up its veins of coal
the mining of the coal from the seam
the carrying of the coal to the saltpans
the collected sea water in the bucket pots
the transferring of the water to the iron pans
the burning of the coal and the heat
the smell of sulphur and the cautioning memory of one explosion
the water rising to the boil
the steam rising from the pans
the coagulant, blood in the water
the careful drawing out of the impurities
the cooling of the pans
the raking of the pans
the pure white crystals of salt that are left
the smoke smell that clings to your clothes
the swelling in your hands
the salt in your skin
the salt on your tongue
the salt and the coal
the earth and the sea.

The Battle of Kringen / Sinklar's Visa

And how would I tell the story?
There is a song already – an inverted telling,
where our men are the enemy, so I suppose there is room
for another version. For we do not believe
that they set out across the heather
with intentions of sin –

the Sinclair tartan has a green background:
the green of the land in summer,
a cool and classic welcoming green,
but green is worn by the Old Folk of the land
and they can take offence
when mortals wear their chosen colour.
In other times, the Sinclair Earl crossed away
from home on a Monday before he fell in battle
and since then no Sinclair should leave that day,
nor wear the green,
but they do.

The green is backed with the warning wave
of the blue sea, shot through with red.

The Scots sailed for three days and
the moon shone in the pale night
and the fourth morning dawned
as they arrived in Norway.

Turn around, turn around
called the sea, before that dawn,
turn around, before your death.

An army does not travel lightly:
waged men of war
cut through a landscape.

Why do men join these expeditions –
in Scotland, there was famine, poverty –
and this was no small adventure
to travel into.

They took a narrow path through unknown country,
past unknown people, who drew back from them
silent and smouldering like the ashes of a smoored fire
ready to rekindle.

As the Scots, that company of pretty men,
came closer into the valley
the staff struck the floor,
the horns of attack sounded –
an attack is not pretty
the Scots had not waited for luck

but ran speeding
headlong to their own destruction
into the boiling blood of others' battles
the rocks rolled down the hillside, smashing
all at the bottom of the steep banks
by the purling stream
like crude earthen pots would smash
if you rolled them downwards
a small image, a thing
miserably cut to pieces with a childish fist –

through the night
the old gods and the new watch the barn
where the survivors lay until morning
grouping, gathering, crowding round
in a kind of hushed anticipation,
feverish with excitement
a waiting pause, a decision, debate on who to sacrifice
whether the sacrifice is enough to keep the land safe,
assuage the need for killing
or too much –

We thought we were the north men
fighting for our small country
here, we were the strangers, the enemy
we can only speak of it with reluctance.
A victor can sing, or a proud loser,
this blinking in the harsh morning light of choice
as the gods hold their breath
at the unfolding of a song
is not a thing to tell easily –

until the storm-king,
closer to men than the gods,
took pity
and slowly, silently
shrouded both the living and the dead
with the cooling snow.

children of ash and elm

the ash tree starts out male like the moon in the islands
the next year she is as female
as the moon over the sea
the dark flowers from the black buds
grow fast, and tall at first,
but soon the root growth overtakes
the visible branches
forcing its way underground
through cracks in the bedrock
demanding the water to match
the near-endless light of early summer
the roots fed, thrumming with life
now lace the island together
twining through the rock.
in the slow-growing upper branches
the gods sit, impassive
as the dieback begins
their thoughts like roots lying deep
as the fungus spreads,
the leaves thinning and lost,
like the hair of an old man –

elm is ailm: it was the first
and last,
the jewel of trees
of the field edge, hedgerow tree
of the prized burrs –
and the tree of the burial ground.
a balance of life and death.
the rich brown of the heartwood
tolerated the bad air
until the unease spread too far
now the internal beetle-scarring
is a badge of birth and pride

fallen leaves and barkless branches
make a skeleton tree
but the roots stretch under houses
creeping green suckers still
renewing each ninth year
but never regaining height
the crown is gone

the wych is native to Scotland
the ash the Scandinavian guardian
in the shadow of the roots we were told
the children of the ash and elm would huddle
ready to start the cycle again

the ash and the elm were a union
a man and a woman in the old creation story
a union like this story of Scotland and Faroe
but now they are united
in reaching the edge of ages together:
they are two trees dying together

we chose
the ash of the moon,
the elm of the sun

we avoided climbing
into trees with no roots:
the grey tangled roots remain –
they are everywhere under our feet –
this was a strength:
now the ground is shifting

to be a child of ash and elm now
is to feel the unease of the world

Horizon Calendar in the Astronomical Twilight

In the evening the stones say breathe:
there is no true night in the summer north
the air hums with life, the stones speak
in the twilight, asking
where are we going?
The answer is in the heart of the stone
under the delicate broken lines of pale pink light
filtered through the leaves and branches of the trees
as the evening dims
stone rough under my palms warm from
the sun beating
down:
There is more.
there is summer and there is life and it goes on
and the circle is as old as we are, no older,
but we are as old as our memories
as old as our stories
as new as the tales we tell to ourselves

Scattered Words

A pale pink rose, a cathedral under the sea
the dance beating in a ring,
the angles and the constant wind
the rain on the wet grass, and
the sheep's wool in the fading light
the children's arms around you as
the smoke and dreams drift up to the rafters
the music and the geese flying overhead and
the stories of the clan in the land below their flight
the burning of the papers and the original Jofrid, watching.
The rock, the violin, the summer, salt and coal
rock violin summer salt coal
song sea oarsmen birds sea sea sea

pale rose cathedral dance ring constant
rain wool light children dream song
rock violin summer stories
song oarsmen birds memory thought life

We are left with a remembrance
of scattered words
memory and thought balanced,
one on each shoulder.

Pale Cathedral Sea Dance Ring Constant
Cathedral Sea Dance Ring Constant Pale
Sea Dance Ring Constant Pale Cathedral
Dance Ring Constant Pale Cathedral Sea
Ring Constant Pale Cathedral Sea Dance
Constant Pale Cathedral Sea Dance Ring

Rain Wool Light Children Dream Song
Wool Light Children Dream Song Rain

Light Children Dream Song Rain Wool
Children Dream Song Rain Wool Light
Dream Song Rain Wool Light Children
Song Rain Wool Light Children Dream

Rock Violin Stories Birds Thought Memory
Violin Stories Birds Thought Memory Rock
Stories Birds Thought Memory Rock Violin
Birds Thought Memory Rock Violin Stories
Thought Memory Rock Violin Stories Birds
Memory Rock Violin Stories Birds Thought

Time Ocean Water Deep

If I could say one thing to that
girl on the shore it would be:
do not worry. There is time.
There is time enough to wait.
Through time, it will not
pass, but it will ease
time water-deep like the ocean.
By the shore your hand raises
to brush a salt drop
ocean spray
and time drifts dangerously tidal
and as you walk away from the shore
I want to run after, calling,
all comfort gone, frantic now,
shouting beware
because I said there was time
there is time
but it is gone so fast
so fast

Open light

What does the world look like from here
from the centre, in spring
with the bright shock of flowers in the soaked earth
the endless changing form of the sea
and the wide wide open light of the sky
and what does it sound like
here in the middle of the world
the soughing of the wind and the battering
of the rain on the roof
and the sea again, birds,
and people and music all inside:
it sounds like the pibroch: unexpectedly right.
The straight intent of the piper
a followed thought, a word to anchor
a rhythm running ahead
a tune that tells of worlds
here in the centre of everything.
Despite the sea's insistence
it is the open sky that takes the memory.

Broken Chronicle

I said I would be my own chronicler
but my life was many people's story
a looping, repeated, standing story
no truth, little import, yet full of life

my husband, children, clan, the land I'm in
the mountains, the sea, the birds overhead
flying, not free, but unfolding patterns
expected, longed for, and misunderstood.

There is sadness for the young girl who
no longer wants to be a warrior
a life takes a long time to live and this
broken sonnet does not hold the answer

but I am still here with my tangled words
that one, by the shore, listening to the sea.

Notes

Lines in Old English poetry have four stresses, two on either side of a caesura: the third stressed word should alliterate with the first or second, or both. It relies heavily on alliteration, rather than rhyme. In Old Norse poetry the unstressed syllables are lost, leaving it very terse. I have used this theory as a starting point for some of the poems in this collection, particularly some of the sonnets.

'Fagra blóma' (Beautiful Flower) is a well-known Faroese song: the words are a poem by Poul F. Joensen and the melody, composed later, is by Hanus G. Johansen. The only true Faroese rose is pink: the Faroese Soft Downy Rose (*Rosa mollis*). It may well have been introduced by the Vikings. It does not flower every year, so when it blooms it is special.

Njal's Saga is one of the great Norse sagas, telling the tragic tale of Njal, who is caught up against his will in blood feuds and family disputes and is eventually burnt alive.

'Thought' and 'Memory' are the names of Odin's ravens ('Huginn' and 'Muninn').

Kennings are a compound noun used for a simple noun, often found in old Scandinavian writing.

The Princess of Nólsoy is a well-known Faroese story, but there is a similar story in Suðuroy. In the Nólsoy story it is not clear which of the six King James of Scotland is meant, though James II and V are both suggested. James V was a notorious womaniser, and the 16th century in Scotland is my own particular historical period of interest. The Clan Gunn lived at that time between Sutherland and Caithness, and their stories feature tangentially in my book *Daughters of the North*. The research I did for *Daughters of the North*, the glimpses of half-remembered stories in the archives, was the start of what became *Jofrid Gunn*.

Skjaldur are a little like nursery rhymes: in the original Faroese they usually rhyme, and often feature birds, animals or the supernatural. Sometimes they tell a story, but often a nonsense story.

The huldufólk are tall and grey; they live hidden but walk among humans in the Faroe Islands. They sound to me similar to the Old Ones – the fairy folk of Scotland, who can be dangerous and unpredictable.

Kvæði are the old ballads of the Faroe Islands. 'Ormurin Langi' by Jens Christian Djurhus provides the rhythm and starting point for 'The Dancing in the Hall'.

Old Norse languages, and Old English, had different letters, including the thorn (Þ) and eth (ð). The eth is used, though mainly silent, in Faroese, and is considered a marker of the language.

Thirsty with nostalgia: I heard a Russian saying 'it happened so long ago, it's not true anymore'.

There are sea stacks, steep, vertical columns of rock in the sea near the coast, in the Faroes and in the Far North of Scotland. Risin and Kellingin in the Faroes are said to be a giant and giantess who were towing the islands north to Iceland.

Feigdarferð is a Faroese word for a journey where you don't reach home, an 'ill-fated journey'. I first heard it in the Hamradun song of the same title.

The national flower in the Faroes is the *sólja*, or buttercup, which grows everywhere on the islands. The *snjósólja*, or snow or glacier buttercup, is a white flower that grows at the top of mountains in the Faroes.

Juniper is the badge of Clan Gunn. Its Gaelic name is *aittin* or *samh*. Samh is associated with *Samhain* or Hallowe'en: juniper was burnt at the entrances of Scottish homes to keep away evil spirits that night. Juniper is also called the mountain yew, and can be found in wet, peaty, acidic hillsides, as far north as Orkney. A slow-growing low shrub with sharp-pointed blue-green aromatic needles, it is found with heather on the moorland, and under old Highland birch and pine woods. Oil from juniper berries flavours gin, and the berries can spice soup, stew or venison. In Sutherland, babies were given teething twigs of Juniper, which were also claimed to provide protection against harm.

The great hammerbeam roof of Darnaway Castle can still be seen. In the time of Mary, Queen of Scots, it was said to hold 1,000 armed men.

Parting hymns were sung when the boats went out fishing. The church bells stopped ringing when people were forbidden to gather because of plague: as with Covid-19.

Trolls frequently occur in Scandinavian stories.

Geese are passage migrants through the Faroes; their breeding grounds are further north e.g. in Iceland or Greenland. Some types of geese winter in Scotland, coming not only from Iceland or Greenland but also Canada and Russia. For a comprehensive yet readable account of birdlife on the Faroes see *The Atlantic Islands* by Kenneth Williamson.

The origins of the Clan Gunn are discussed in Robert Gordon's *Genealogical History of the Earldom of Sutherland*, along with many of their stories as they interacted with the Gordons, Sinclairs and Mackays in the 16th and 17th centuries. The Clan were said to be descended from Gun, the king of Denmark's son, who settled in Caithness. The original rhyme about the different families in the north of Scotland runs "Sinclair, Sutherland, Keith and Clan Gun; Never was peace where these four were in". This rhyme can be found, among other places, in the *History of the Clan Mackay*. In the later time of the Clearances, people rented their houses and lands, but owned the roof beams so could take them away if they moved.

'Burial party' was partly inspired by the sometimes dark paintings of Sámal Joensen-Mikines.

Creagh-Drumi-Doun was a 1579 foray led by new Mackay chief Uisdean against the Clan Gunn, in revenge for the Gunns' dependence on the Earls of Sutherland. Uisdean was backed by the Earl of Caithness, who had no love for the Sutherlands. Uisdean's leadership of the Mackay clan was contested, and his half-brother John Beg was 'much offended' that Uisdean had not respected a Mackay alliance with the Gunns. Sutherland took reprisals against the Mackays, killing many of them and taking back their booty to be dispersed among the Clan Gunn. Later, John Beg was killed, and the Clan Gunn maintained a feud against the clans that harboured his killers. John Beg's killing was convenient for Uisdean, and slightly obscure: another branch of the Mackay clan, the Abrach Mackays, may have been involved, and may have been supported by the Earl of Caithness. The name Creagh-Drumi-Doun is obscure, but seems to be a mix of Gaelic and Scots that gives us an image of the noise of a fierce raid as drums were beaten and men charged downhill. The name Creagh-Drumi-Doun is an interesting mix of Gaelic and Scots (showing the way those languages mixed in the Far North). Some of the names of the protagonists are likewise difficult to identify, such as the Slaight-Ean-Aberigh (possibly the 'host, or people, of Ian Abrach'), who were involved in the killing of John Beg. Information for the battle is found in only one source (Robert Gordon), and even that source, usually so detailed, acknowledges that the meaning for part of the feuding is very obscure – though the author may have been masking his own family's involvement.

Blowing froth from an offered drink was supposed to help avoid witchcraft, according to old stories in the Faroes.

Votive ships are models of ships displayed in churches. They are seen in the Faroes and also in Scotland.

The original Jofrid appears in three Icelandic sagas: her first appearance in *Hen-Thorir* caught my attention and is one of the original inspirations for these poems: "Jofrid had a tent pitched for her out of doors, finding this less dull." Thorodd Tungu-Oddson meets her there and is equally taken with her; despite their families being at odds, they marry. However, Thorodd hears that his brother Thorvald has been taken captive in Scotland and sails to rescue him. Neither Thorodd nor his brother return. Jofrid Gunnarsdottir then marries Thorstein Egilsson of Borg, "and proved a most remarkable lady." Jofrid and her daughter appear again in the saga of the poet "Gunnlaug Wormtongue", and Jofrid and her second husband are also mentioned briefly in the story of Jofrid's father-in-law *Egil's Saga*. Jofrid's second husband Thorstein was "an exceptionally handsome man", but he and Jofrid did not get on with Egil. Jofrid had ten children with Thorstein, and "their line of descent… was a great one, and included many people of distinction", including poets.

Shielings are temporary shelters used by shepherds and herdsmen in summer grazing. The word is close to words meaning 'hiding place', 'shelter' and 'hut'.

Robert Gordon's burning of the papers of the earl of Caithness is one of the great historical destructions in the Far North, which wiped out the written history of the Sinclairs. Robert himself tells the story in his *Genealogical History of the Earldom of Sutherland* and there is an analysis in Ian Grimble's *Chief of Mackay*. The incident features in my own book *Daughters of the North*.

'He wrote asking for a suit of scarlet and grey' is based on a letter from Alexander, Knight of Navidale, to his brother Robert Gordon, the Tutor of Sutherland. The letter is printed in the Sutherland Book, Volume 2. The original is in Scots.

Lammastide is the 1st of August. One of the traditional Scottish quarter days, it is also an old point of contact between the agricultural world and the Church. Lammas was a Pagan festival of Celtic origin. Crops are harvested at this time, and it was customary to bring a loaf of bread, made from the new crop, to church as an offering to be blessed. The Scots words used are translated as follows:

> Tealzeour = tailor
> Siller = silver
> Coitt = coat
> Tocher = to provide with a dowry.
> Tocherit his dochteris = gave his daughters a dowry.
> Quhilk = which, what

Some of 'A plea…' is inspired by the letter from Donald Mackay, Chief of Mackay, to his grandmother Jean Gordon, Countess of Sutherland, in which Donald discusses his difficult relationship with his uncle Robert (Jean's son) (Sutherland book, vol 2, 129-30. Letter 136. Sir Donald Mackay to Jane, Countess of Sutherland, his grandmother, – wishing to have disputes settled. 5th May 1617). Donald has a particular turn of phrase; distinctively of its time and place (the Far North of Scotland), with a visible influence from Gaelic.

There are many northern traditions of boat burning; the most well-known is Up Helly Aa in Shetland.

The Faroe Islands supposedly had no musical instruments until someone brought a violin there in the 1860s, partly because of their remoteness and partly because of the trade monopoly which was in place. Singing and chain dancing were popular. Violins and music are integral to William

Heinemann's classic Faroese novel *The Lost Musicians*. In the 16th century, fiddles were not quite the instrument we know today, but an early version was known in Scotland: Mary, Queen of Scots was welcomed to Edinburgh by a group of local people serenading her by singing and playing on fiddles. She thought the noise was dreadful, but was polite to them.

Jean Gordon, Countess of Sutherland, started the successful coal mine and salt pan in Brora in the 16th century: an early example of industrialisation in the north Highlands. Oxblood or egg white is used as a coagulant in the salt-making process: the other matter sits on the surface of the water and draws the impurities (such as pieces of shell or seaweed) towards it. The salt maker continually skims the water, taking out the impurities and the coagulant together to leave the pure salt.

'Sinklar's Visa' is a Norwegian song, telling the true story of the death of Caithness mercenaries at the hands of Norwegian peasants. One of the real Sinclairs was fostered with the Clan Gunn. A contemporary telling of the story is found in Robert Gordon's *A Genealogical History of the Earldom of Sutherland*. The song became associated with nationalism, and is particularly popular in the Faroe Islands, where it has been reinterpreted in modern heavy metal versions. The superstition about Sinclair men not wearing green is mentioned in Calder's *History of Caithness*, but it is not limited to the Sinclairs: green is the colour of the dress the fairies wore, and they were supposed to take offence when mortals wore it.

Dutch Elm disease and Ash dieback are decimating trees across the UK. It has taken a while for the diseases to spread to the north of the country, but each is irreversible and unstoppable. In Norse mythology, the first man and woman were made from driftwood found on the shore – the man was ash and the woman elm. Yggdrasil, 'The World Tree', is an ash tree. When Ragnarök (the end of the world) comes, a man and a woman who hide in the tree survive to start the new cycle. Ash trees can switch sex from year to year. In Faroese the word for the moon is gendered male – in other European languages e.g. French, the moon is female. Elm is 'ailm', the first letter of the Gaelic tree alphabet. 'Choose the ash of the shade…' is a line from *Carmina Gadelica*.

Singing stones: there are many stories of speaking or singing stones and mysterious stone circles in the north.